Up
Close
and GROSS
Microscopic Creatures

DISGUSTING
FOOD INVADERS

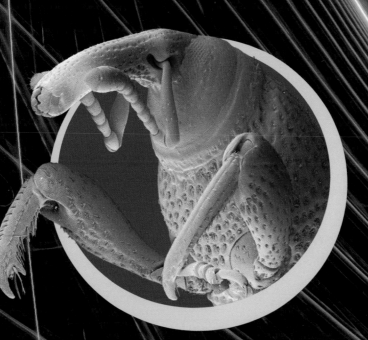

by Ruth Owen

Consultant: Suzy Gazlay, M.A.
Recipient, Presidential Award
for Excellence in Science Teaching

BEARPORT
PUBLISHING

New York, New York

Credits

Cover, © Power and Syred/Science Photo Library; CoverBKG, © Geanina Bechea/ Shutterstock; 3, © Clouds Hill Imaging/www.lastrefuge.co.uk; 4, © Scimat/Science Photo Library; 5, © Steve Gschmeissner/Science Photo Library; 6, © Shutterstock; 7, © Power and Syred/Science Photo Library; 8, © Scott Bauer/U.S. Department of Agriculture/Science Photo Library; 9, © Volker Steger/Science Photo Library; 10, © Pascal Goetgheluck/Science Photo Library; 11, © Clouds Hill Imaging/www. lastrefuge.co.uk; 12, © Horia Bogdan/Shutterstock; 13, © Dr. Jeremy Burgess/ Science Photo Library; 14, © Pascal Goetgheluck/Science Photo Library; 15, © Biophoto Associates/Science Photo Library; 16L, © Matka Wariatka/Shutterstock; 16R, © Shutterstock; 17, © Susumu Nishinaga/Science Photo Library; 18T, © Shutterstock; 18B, © Susan Ellis/Bugwood.org; 19, © Aranya Edmonds; 20, © Dr. Jeremy Burgess/Science Photo Library; 21, © Stephanie Schuller/Science Photo Library; 22, © Susumu Nishinaga/Science Photo Library.

Publisher: Kenn Goin
Editorial Director: Adam Siegel
Creative Director: Spencer Brinker
Design: Alix Wood
Photo Researcher: Ruby Tuesday Books Ltd

Library of Congress Cataloging-in-Publication Data

Owen, Ruth.
  Disgusting food invaders / by Ruth Owen.
     p. cm. — (Up close and gross: microscopic creatures)
  Includes bibliographical references and index.
  ISBN-13: 978-1-61772-126-7 (library binding)
  ISBN-10: 1-61772-126-3 (library binding)
  1. Foodborne diseases—Juvenile literature. 2. Parasites—Juvenile literature.
  3. Plant parasites—Juvenile literature. I. Title. II. Series.

  QR201.F62O94 2011
  615.9'54—dc22

                              2010044417

Published in the United States of America by Bearport Publishing Company, Inc.

For more information, write to Bearport Publishing Company, Inc., 101 Fifth Avenue, Suite 6R, New York, New York 10003. Printed in the United States of America in North Mankato, Minnesota.

122010
10810CGF

10 9 8 7 6 5 4 3 2 1

Contents

What's Eating Your Lunch?

A piece of fruit or cheese is not just a tasty snack for a person. It can also be a meal for hundreds, or even thousands, of tiny food **invaders**.

Some of these creatures, such as insects called thrips, are big enough to see with just your eyes—if you look very carefully. Others, such as **bacteria**, are so small that you need a **microscope** to see them clearly.

In this book you will have a chance to see amazing images of some tiny food invaders. Using a powerful microscope, scientists have zoomed in on these living things to show them up close and in great detail. So get ready to be shocked. You will finally be able to see the thousands of little creatures that are sharing your lunch!

Bacteria

The bacteria on this lettuce leaf could give a person food poisoning. That is why people should always wash fruit and vegetables before eating them. The bacteria are shown 2,700 times their real size!

Thrip

Grass seed

Thrips feed on juice from vegetables, fruits, flowers, and other parts of plants. So be careful when biting into a strawberry. If it hasn't been washed you might be eating some tiny thrips that are on the fruit's skin.

This tiny thrip is feeding among grass seeds. The thrip is just .04 inches (1 mm) long.

Fruit Fly Invasion

The tiny, dot-like fruit fly is an insect that often lays its eggs on ripe or rotting fruit and vegetables. These foods are the perfect meal for the fly's young when they **hatch**.

A female fruit fly will lay up to 500 **microscopic** eggs on a piece of fruit such as a ripe banana. In less than 24 hours, hundreds of tiny **larvae**, or **maggots**, hatch from the eggs and start eating the fruit. During the next six days or so, the worm-like larvae grow and change as they become adults. These new flies are ready to **reproduce** right away, and in just over a week, their young will become adults, too! This means the original fly and her eggs can quickly become an invasion of thousands!

These ripe bananas will quickly attract fruit flies.

A bowl filled with fruit is not the only place where a female fruit fly can lay her eggs. A garbage disposal that has slimy pieces of fruit in it or a sticky splash of juice under a refrigerator are both good places for a fly's larvae to find a meal once they hatch.

This fruit fly is landing on a banana.
The fly can flap its wings about 220 times in a second!

Moths in Your Cornflakes

The Indian meal moth is a tiny insect that invades kitchen cabinets where food is stored. Female moths lay their eggs near foods that their young can feed on, such as cereal, pasta, and dried fruit. When a moth's tiny young, or larvae, hatch from their eggs, they may squeeze into a box of cereal or pasta through the places where the cardboard edges join together. Once inside, the larvae eat and grow bigger—sometimes for many months.

Finally, each larva spins a silk covering called a cocoon. Inside the cocoon the larva becomes a **pupa**. This is the stage of the insect's life when it changes into an adult moth. People may not know that their food has been invaded until they open a box of cereal and a cloud of moths flutter out!

An Indian meal moth larva eating cereal

As they feed and move around, Indian meal moth larvae produce silk threads that look like cobwebs. They leave these webs in cabinets and over the foods they invade.

This adult Indian meal moth is sitting on a raisin. The moth is just 3/8 inch (1 cm) long.

Cheese-Chomping Cheese Mites

If a block of cheese looks like it is covered with gray dust, think twice before you take a bite. Instead of eating the cheese, watch the dust closely. If you start to see it move around, then you'll know the dust isn't actually dust at all. It's thousands of tiny cheese mites!

Cheese mites are microscopic, eight-legged creatures that are related to spiders. Once they find a block of cheese, the mites will eat their way into it. The gray, dust-like layer that can be seen on the surface of the cheese includes living mites, dead mites, mite body parts, and cheese mite poop!

Some cheese makers put cheese mites on their cheese on purpose. Why? As the mites munch on the cheese, they leave **digestive juices** on it. Some people like the flavor that the juices give the cheese.

A cheese maker sprinkling cheese mites onto blocks of cheese

A cheese mite is smaller than the period at the end of this sentence.

A Mold Sandwich

People don't know this food invader has arrived until they decide to make a sandwich. Then disaster strikes! After taking a slice of bread from a bag, they'll soon see that it is covered in patches of hairy **mold**!

Mold is a type of **fungus**. Fungi are living things that spread by releasing microscopic **particles** called **spores** into the air. Thousands of fungi spores are around us all the time. They float in the air until they land on the right place to grow into new fungi.

When bread fungus spores land on bread, they quickly grow into new fungi and start releasing more spores. Within a few days, a slice of bread can become covered with mold!

People should not eat food with mold on it because some kinds are poisonous and can make humans very ill. Moldy food should always be thrown away.

Mold

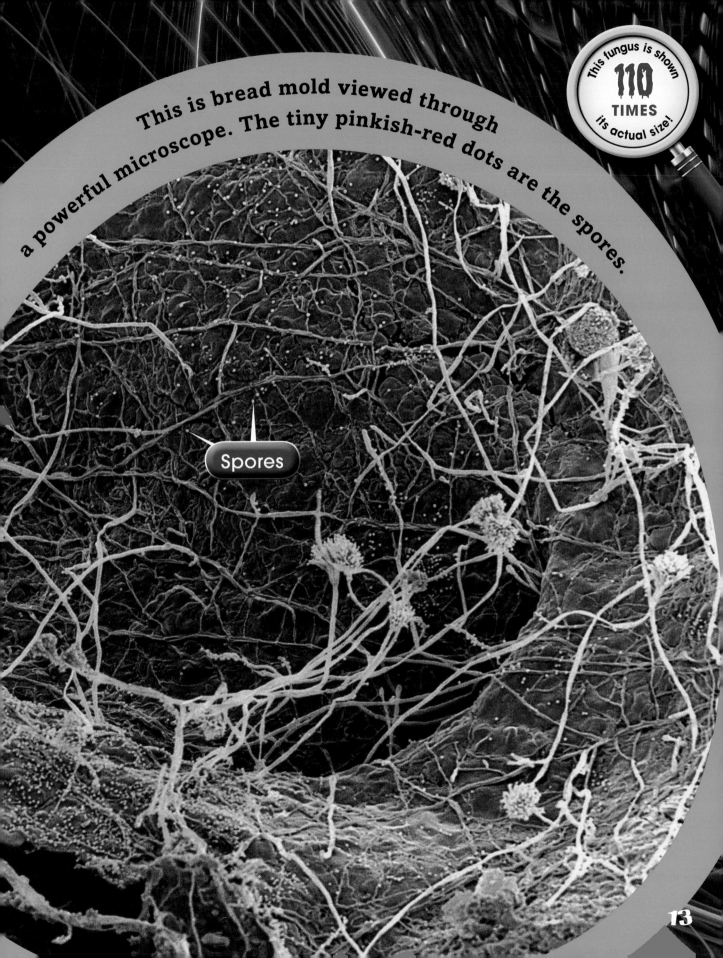

This is bread mold viewed through a powerful microscope. The tiny pinkish-red dots are the spores.

This fungus is shown **110** TIMES its actual size!

Spores

Grain-Eating Grubs

Grain weevils are insects that invade the buildings where grains such as wheat, oats, rice, and corn are stored. Weevils eat the grain and also leave their eggs behind in it.

A female weevil makes a hole in a grain of wheat or rice using her cutting mouthparts. Then she lays a single egg inside the grain and blocks up the hole using her sticky **saliva**. A female grain weevil can lay about 200 eggs in her lifetime.

A tiny larva, called a grub, hatches from each egg. The grub feeds on the inside of the grain as it grows and changes into an adult weevil. The weevil then makes a hole in the grain, crawls out, and begins its adult life.

Sometimes tons of grain have to be destroyed because they have been invaded by grain weevils. The grain can no longer be used to make foods such as bread or breakfast cereal.

This scientist is testing for grain weevils. He is using equipment that picks up sounds from the insects.

Cutting mouthparts

Wheat grain

This grain weevil climbs out of the wheat grain where it has grown from a larva into an adult.

A Peanut Butter and Rat Hair Sandwich

Anyone hungry for a peanut butter and rat hair sandwich? It sounds gross, but people eat rat hairs, bits of bugs, and even specks of animal poop all the time. They just don't know it.

Insects and other animals such as rats like to eat the same kinds of foods that humans do. As a result, they find ways to sneak into places where products such as peanut butter are made and stored. Food producers could kill the invaders with chemicals. However, the food would then have chemicals on it, too—which would harm people more than eating parts of the invaders. The fact is that a rat hair or an ant leg in a peanut butter sandwich won't hurt a person, and the peanut butter still tastes good. Right?

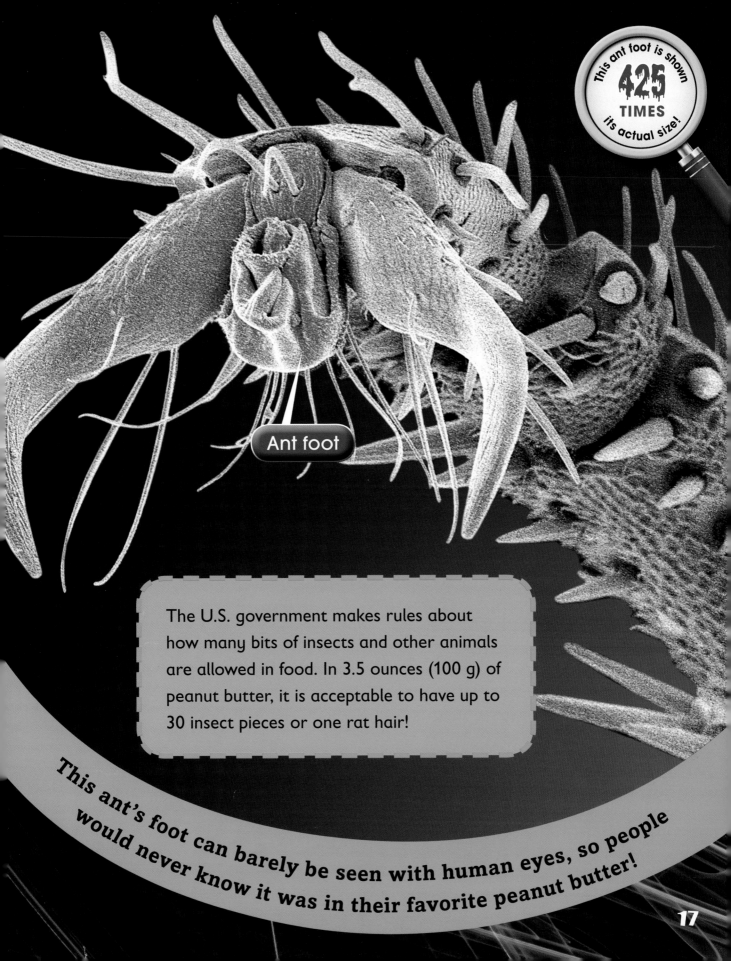

Ant foot

The U.S. government makes rules about how many bits of insects and other animals are allowed in food. In 3.5 ounces (100 g) of peanut butter, it is acceptable to have up to 30 insect pieces or one rat hair!

This ant's foot can barely be seen with human eyes, so people would never know it was in their favorite peanut butter!

Maggot Cheese, Anyone?

On the Italian island of Sardinia, people have been eating an unusual cheese for hundreds of years. The cheese is called Casu Marzu (KAH-soo MAR-zoo), which means "rotten cheese." It is made with the help of wiggly fly larvae called maggots!

A cheese called pecorino is left outside and uncovered. Flies, called cheese flies, land on the cheese and lay their eggs on it. Maggots hatch and eat the cheese. As they eat, their digestive juices get onto the cheese and make it soft. The juices also give the cheese a strong taste that some people like. The flavor is so strong that it burns the tongue. Some people remove the maggots from the cheese before eating it. Others don't!

Pecorino cheese before the maggots start eating

An adult cheese fly on the surface of pecorino cheese

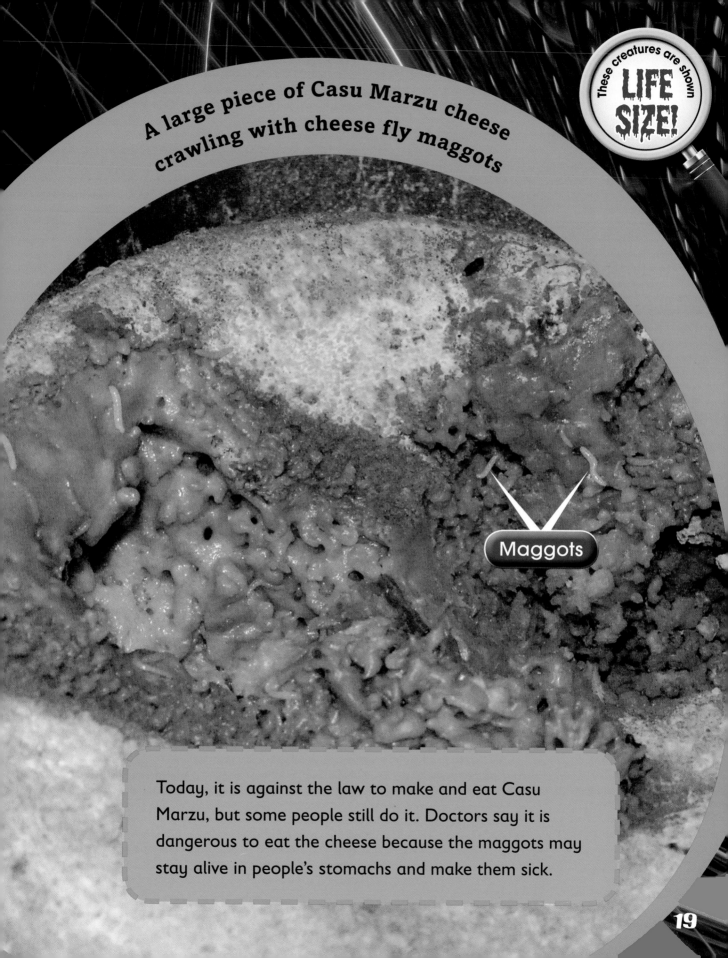

A large piece of Casu Marzu cheese crawling with cheese fly maggots

These creatures are shown **LIFE SIZE!**

Maggots

Today, it is against the law to make and eat Casu Marzu, but some people still do it. Doctors say it is dangerous to eat the cheese because the maggots may stay alive in people's stomachs and make them sick.

Bacteria – Microscopic Food Invaders

Some of the most dangerous food invaders are bacteria. Humans cannot see these microscopic living things, but some types of bacteria can make people very sick if they eat them.

Two common types of bacteria that cause food poisoning are **Salmonella** and **E. coli**. They often live on poop and on animals. People might get these bacteria on their hands when they go to the bathroom or pet an animal. The bacteria can then be transferred to food. After eating the bacteria, people may have stomach pains, vomiting, and **diarrhea**.

People should always wash their hands with warm water and soap before touching food. This will help remove harmful bacteria.

Bacteria

Roast beef

These *Salmonella* bacteria were carried from some animal poop on the body of a fly to this slice of roast beef.

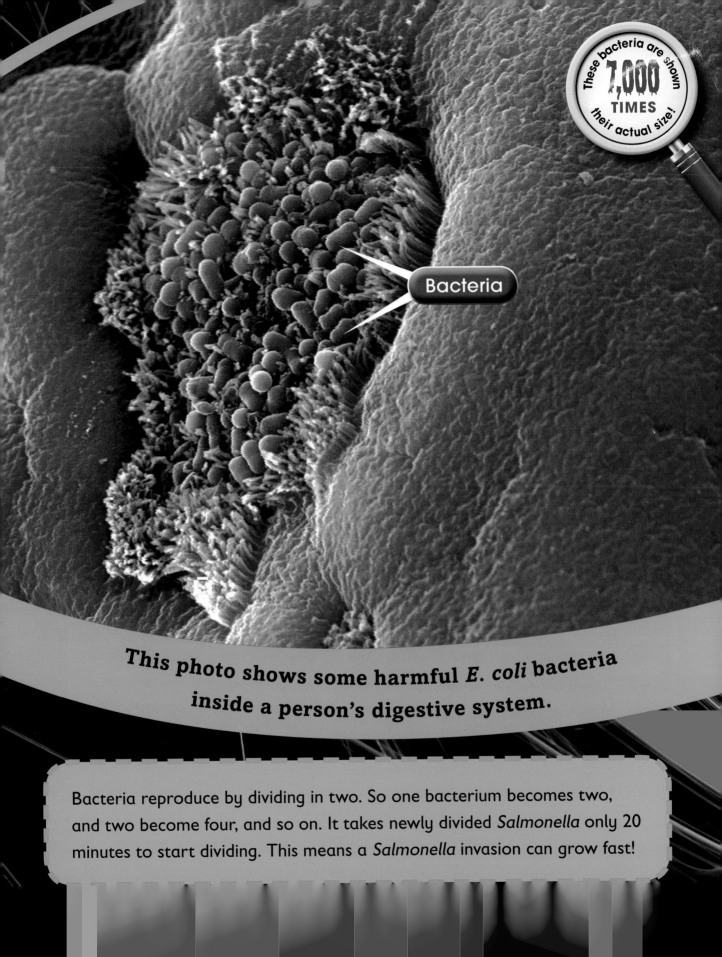

These bacteria are shown **7,000 TIMES** their actual size!

Bacteria

This photo shows some harmful *E. coli* bacteria inside a person's digestive system.

Bacteria reproduce by dividing in two. So one bacterium becomes two, and two become four, and so on. It takes newly divided *Salmonella* only 20 minutes to start dividing. This means a *Salmonella* invasion can grow fast!

Getting Up Close

The amazing close-up photographs in this book were created using a very powerful microscope. It is called a scanning **electron** microscope, or SEM.

Microscopes make things look bigger. A scanning electron microscope can show what things look like hundreds of times their real size.

How were the photos in this book created?

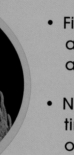

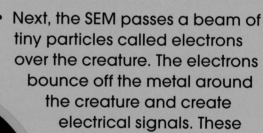

- First, a creature is covered with a super-thin layer of metal, such as gold.

- Next, the SEM passes a beam of tiny particles called electrons over the creature. The electrons bounce off the metal around the creature and create electrical signals. These signals are turned into a black-and-white image of the creature on a computer.

- Scientists then add color to the SEM image using a computer.

Glossary

bacteria (bak-TEER-ee-uh) tiny living things that can be seen only with a microscope; some bacteria are helpful and keep humans and animals healthy; some bacteria are harmful and cause disease; singular form is *bacterium*

diarrhea (*dye*-uh-REE-uh) runny, watery body waste that makes a person need to go to the bathroom many times

digestive juices (dye-JES-tiv JOO-siz) liquids in the mouth, stomach, and other parts of the digestive system that help break down food so that the body can use it for fuel

E. coli (EE KOH-lye) a bacterium found in the intestines of humans and other warm-blooded animals; *E. coli* is usually harmless and aids in digestion, but some forms of it can cause food poisoning and other digestive problems

electron (i-LEK-tron) a tiny particle that is found in atoms, the building blocks of all matter; electrons carry electrical charges

fungus (FUHN-guhss) a living thing that is neither a plant nor an animal; mushrooms and mold are types of fungi; plural form is *fungi*

hatch (HACH) to come out of an egg

invaders (in-VAYD-urz) living things that enter a place where they don't normally belong

larvae (LAR-vee) the worm-like form of many kinds of young insects; singular form is *larva*

maggots (MAG-uhts) the larvae, or worm-like young, of flies

microscope (MYE-kruh-skohp) a tool used to see things that are too small to see with the eyes alone

microscopic (*mye*-kroh-SKOP-ik) able to be seen only with a microscope

mold (MOHLD) a living thing that is neither a plant nor an animal and that grows in old food and on damp surfaces; it is a type of fungus

particles (PAR-ti-kuhlz) tiny pieces

pupa (PYOO-puh) the stage in the life cycle of some insects during which the insect changes from a larva to an adult

reproduce (*ree*-pruh-DOOSS) to produce more of a living thing such as an animal, plant, fungus, or bacterium

saliva (suh-LYE-vuh) a clear liquid produced in the mouths of humans and many animals that helps them swallow and chew; also called *spit*

Salmonella (*sal*-muh-NEL-uh) a bacterium that can live inside and outside of the body and is transmitted on food and waste matter; it can cause a variety of illnesses, including diarrhea

spores (SPORZ) tiny structures that are produced by many living things, such as some types of plants and fungi; spores are able to become new individuals of that life form

Index

Bibliography

U.S. Food and Drug Administration: *http://www.fda.gov.*

Warren, Adrian. *Unseen Companions: Big Views of Tiny Creatures.* Wells, Somerset, UK: Last Refuge Ltd. (2007).

Read More

Goldish, Meish. *Baby Bug Dishes (Extreme Cuisine).* New York: Bearport Publishing (2009).

Maynard, Christopher. *Micro Monsters: Life Under the Microscope.* New York: DK Publishing (1999).

Nguyen, Nam. *Micro Monsters.* New York: Kingfisher (2010).

Learn More Online

To learn more about food invaders, visit
www.bearportpublishing.com/UpCloseandGross

About the Author

Ruth Owen has been writing children's books for more than ten years. She lives in Cornwall, England, just minutes from the ocean. Ruth loves gardening and caring for her family of llamas.